Prophetic Utterance

Minister Verleiz Lattimore, Prophetess

When God Speaks it is for us to listen, hear, discern and move in obedience. Trust God first and foremost.

Prophetic Utterance

Minister Verleiz Lattimore, Prophetess

Any true prophet will send you back to God. This book is meant to encourage you through the prophetic word to seek God for His guidance and direction in your life. Mediate on the words given and see what God is saying to you through the word. Everyone will connect differently but you will also connect correctly if you seek God first.

God is Your Strength

The word of the Lord is:

"Today is a day where you will look within for answers to complex situations, be slow to anger, as God will be your strength."

Season of Promotion

The word of the Lord is:

"Promotion comes in a season of focus and listening. You want to listen to that which is said and that which is not said. I cover you as I move you through to your promotion."

Don't Second Guess

The word of the Lord is:

"Favor is coming your way. Don't second guess your decisions. You will see the turnaround in something small but worth counting."

Let ME into Your Heart

The word of the Lord is:

"Let ME into your heart and home in this season and see the wonders I set at your door. New money, new transportation, new careers are all on the table before thee. Let ME into your prayers."

Peace and Newness

The word of the Lord is:

"Peace be with you as you start something new this week. Don't take no for an answer. God has already prepared your yes."

Transformation in Your Mind

The word of the Lord is:

"Transformation in your mind will cause relationships in your life to shift and change, but worry not. I will be with you. This is for your greater good."

Hopes and Dreams

The word of the Lord is:

"The best has yet to come. You are entering a time where your hopes and dreams are a step away. Don't give up."

Travel and Relationships

The word of the Lord is:

"Travel shall be your portion, get ready to make new moves and to see new things. Right relationships will promote the greatest opportunities."

Open Your Mind

The word of the Lord is:

"Money is seeking you. Open your mind to an increase like you have never known before."

Know When to Relax

The word of the Lord is:

"Deeper revelation shall be yours in this season. You are making a way for the success I have promised you. Learn to know when to relax. Remove the distractions."

Test MY Word

The word of the Lord is:

"No one can stand in the way of the blessing I have called forth for you today. Step out and test the word in your life."

New Ideas

The word of the Lord is:

"I place MY hand upon you in this season for new ideas. Release your fears and move forward in favor. Signed contracts will reveal MY promises to you in unexpected ways. I give you permission to laugh again, it is long overdue."

New Chapter

The word of the Lord is:

"Welcome to the new chapter in your life. Let go of the old and make way for the new."

Knowledge and Change

The word of the Lord is:

"Powerful knowledge is your portion. A knowing in your spirit will open up change that will carry you to new levels of truth."

Career and Opportunity

The word of the Lord is:

"Today is a day of new beginnings in career. Seek a new opportunity. I have gone ahead and paved the way."

Pray for Thy Enemies

The word of the Lord is:

"Wish no harm to others but pray even for thy enemy for it is through all that I will bless you in this season. No door is empty of MY promise."

Next in Line for a Blessing

The word of the Lord is:

"You are next line for a blessing. You have considered changing your mind about an opportunity, I say stand. I will bless you in the right hour."

Trust Your Timing

The word of the Lord is:

"Trust your timing for I am with you, leading the way to expansion and new ideas. Right connections are coming to help you finish what has been started. Organization is key in this season."

Measuring for a Blessing

The word of the Lord is:

"I am measuring you in this season for a blessing. Walk toward ME, look not to the right or left but keep your eyes stayed on ME."

Set Up For the Breakthrough

The word of the Lord is:

"Get ready for a move of MY spirit like never before. What looked like a collapsing house of cards was really MY set up for your breakthrough. Accept the challenge to believe and I will meet thee in that secret place where MY secrets are revealed."

Hold Your Peace

The word of the Lord is:

"Hold your peace. I will speak for thee in your time of need and great shall be the outcome. Trust in I, The Lord God."

Seek MY Face and Your Calling

The word of the Lord is:

"Seek MY face and MY calling on your life. I have given you a gift and an assignment. Walk in the path I have set for you and see the great reward that awaits."

Cast Your Worries

The word of the Lord is:

"Progress will come in an important decision. Cast your worries aside."

A Season of Fresh Oil

The word of the Lord is:

"A fresh oil is following from MY house in this season. I have blessed few to receive from this pouring out but those that believe in MY name will know that I have set them aside for such a time as this to walk under the flow of the anointing and the pouring out."

Ask and Receive

The word of the Lord is:

"I am pleased with thee. Ask and you shall receive."

Gift of the Obedient

The word of the Lord is:

"What have you to offer in this season? Have you proved your offering worthy? Have you listened for what I have asked you for or are you giving what you want? Trust comes in obedience and love. Bless the heart of the cheerful giver."

Discern What You Hear

The word of the Lord is:

"Travel will be necessary to clear up a matter. Use discernment with words spoken in your ear."

You Are a Shining Star

The word of the Lord is:

"Stars don't hide they shine and it is the season for you to come out and shine. Listen for MY instructions and I will show you the way up and out. The clouds are moving back to reveal you. "

Protection

The word of the Lord is:

"Be mindful of the company you keep. I am placing a hedge of protection around you and the family."

Check the Mirror

The word of the Lord is:

"Check the mirror, do you see who I have called you to be or who the world has named you to be. I call MY beloved forward for I have made you in MY image and in MY glory."

Great is The Anointing

The word of the Lord is:

"Get ready for the next level. Great is the anointing I am placing around thee."

Brighter Days

The word of the Lord is:

"Brighter days are ahead. I heal thy spirit and maketh thee whole walk in the knowing that I am with thee."

Property and Increase

The word of the Lord is:

"There is property that has your name on it. Get ready for a season of increase. I will show you the land of milk and honey."

Demonstrate His Glory

The word of the Lord is:

"Demonstrate MY glory and power and I will show you great things in your house, your health, and your family situation."

No Weapon

The word of the Lord is:

"No weapon formed shall prosper against thee. Walk in your favor as you overcome the obstacle I have given you victory over."

It Is Time

The word of the Lord is:

"Capture your ideas in writing in this season and watch ME bring them to life. It's time to move forward."

Greater Faith

The word of the Lord is:

"Your faith is making a comeback in greater and greater capacity. You will see the possible in the impossible as MY hand moves in your life."

Practice What You Preach

The word of the Lord is:

"Practice what you preach. Be mindful where you are dropping your gems in this season not all are ready or willing to hear. I will show you where your wisdom is needed."

Unexpected Transportation

The word of the Lord is:

"Transportation favor is awarded to you and the family. Get ready for the unexpected."

Reach For the Stars

The word of the Lord is:

"Reach for the stars and I shall give you beyond. This is your season to do the impossible, stretch."

New Energy, New Blessing

The word of the Lord is:

"You are channeling energy to carry you to into a new blessing. Keep an open mind."

Prophetic Destination

The word of the Lord is:

"Be ready to start something fresh and new. You will not take pieces of the old to start this new venture. A fresh wind is being blown, move with the wind of MY spirit. I shall lead you to your prophetic destination."

Releasing Lack

The word of the Lord is:

"You are releasing lack in this hour. Money shall visit in unexpected abundance. Be it according to your faith."

Clarity and Answers

The word of the Lord is:

"Clarity comes to the man of God who has been seeking in this season. Your prayers have been answered. A family squabble is being resolved."

Nothing Is Impossible

The word of the Lord is:

"Nothing is impossible to you. You are walking into a time of new favor and joy. Laughter shall be your medicine."

Rejoice In a New Day

The word of the Lord is:

"Trust in MY voice in this season. Things won't always be this way. You can rejoice in knowing that I am releasing you into a new day."

Rest and Take Time to Relax

The word of the Lord is:

"Rest today, take time to relax.
There is a reward in the silence that
will show MY peace and increase
your health, joy and wealth."

Results in Your Actions

The word of the Lord is:

"Press in, in this season. You will see results in your actions as you take time to evaluate. Know the joy of a planned miracle. Take time to plan and then act. I will meet you with victory."

Reassurance and Relief

The word of the Lord is:

"I bring you reassurance and new relief. Trust your favor and step out of your comfort zone. I will place you in the right place at the right time."

Discernment in Your Walk

The word of the Lord is:

"If they can't walk with you in the dark they have not been called to walk with you in the light. Use your discernment."

Come Closer

The word of the Lord is:

"Come closer in this season and see MY hand in your life like never before. I have new secrets to share with you that will bring you joy."

Prayer Is Your Answer

The word of the Lord is:

"Prayer is the answer you have been seeking. Seek ME in your prayer time and you will see release."

Respect and Abundance

The word of the Lord is:

"Abundance brings a level of respect to your value. Respect that which I've placed in you and watch your abundance release."

Increase and Favor

The word of the Lord is:

"Know that I have set a plan for your increase and favor. You are walking into a transformation that can't be stopped. Know that MY spirit is in and with you."

Season of More

The word of the Lord is:

"This is a season of more. Place your faith in MY spirit and see the more I have promised you."

Come Forth

The word of the Lord is:

"Place your faith not in others but in ME. I am speaking in this season to bring you out. Come forth."

Patience of the Heart

The word of the Lord is:

"Patience will allow the heart to grow fonder. I have not forgotten MY promise, but your patience will allow you to enjoy the reward so much more."

Refresh and Replenish

The word of the Lord is:

"You shall be refreshed through MY spirit. Manifest in this season as I replenish you. Let MY voice be your guide."

Goodness and Mercy

The word of the Lord is:

"I blow a fresh wind upon thy house. I breathe healing into your situation and understanding of MY goodness and mercy."

New Awakening

The word of the Lord is:

"This is a new awakening. I gave you strength in this last leg of your journey and you will walk out not even smelling of smoke."

Love and Increase

The word of the Lord is:

"Flesh of MY flesh, blood of MY blood, a new anointing shall bless you in MY love and increase. Know that you are MINE and I cherish thee with MY heart."

Laughter is Medicine

The word of the Lord is:

"Transformation in your ideas will walk you into a new season of joy. Laughter shall be medicine to you and you will share your medicine to heal others. Laughter and healing in this season laugh and heal."

Song of MY Joy

The word of the Lord is:

"Let the music play in the heavens to sing of MY joy in you. Apple of MY eye, I have chosen you for greatness. I give new rewards for your obedience."

Raining Blessings

The word of the Lord is:

"I am raining blessings in your life. Know that it is ME the source of your life and rejoice. Don't be afraid to rejoice for this is MY doing."

Fresh Start

The word of the Lord is:

"Swipe out the old and make way for the new. It is your time for a fresh start. I release you into a new season. See your hearts desires and watch them manifest."

Guiding You

The word of the Lord is:

"Don't second guess yourself in this season. I am causing you to be prosperous and take on more. You will begin to feel MY spirit guiding you."

Trust your Dreams

The word of the Lord is:

"New money shall be in your possession. You will see MY hand like never before. Trust the truth in your dreams and seek ME in your heart."

Voice Your Opinion

The word of the Lord is:

"Voicing your opinions in this season will bring you a new prospective of how to see others and how others see you."

Transformation Starts Today

The word of the Lord is:

"Transformation starts today as you have an understanding of ME. Seek ME in your prayers and honor ME in your praises."

What Is In Your Hands

The word of the Lord is:

"Work with what is in your hands. I am bringing you a turn around. You will find perfection in ME for I create all things; I say all things perfect."

Praise with Your Heart

The word of the Lord is:

"With thine heart praise MY name and I will reveal to you the path for this journey you seek. I will be with you along the way and will guide you to victory."

Hear MY Voice

The word of the Lord is:

"Will you not hear MY voice? I have given you options. Take these options set before you and start the change I have designed."

Joyful Instructions

The word of the Lord is:

"When I whisper, I whisper joyful instructions. Follow MY voice and you will conquer sorrow. Trust."

Don't Fear

The word of the Lord is:

"Don't be afraid to try. I am with you and I will place favor before and after you."

Anointed Victory

The word of the Lord is:

"Fresh anointing I give onto you. Set forward in your tasks today knowing I have gone before thee and guaranteed your victory."

Season to Stretch

The word of the Lord is:

"Stretch in this season and try something new. You will see MY hand of favor move to guide your success, I am leading you and giving you stress relievers."

Press into Your Favor

The word of the Lord is:

"Press into your favor and step into the light. This is your moment to start something new and see right results. Walk it out."

Words Match Your Heart

The word of the Lord is:

"Let your words match your heart and you will see the desired results. Know in your heart that I will grant this to thee and you will see."

New Secrets

The word of the Lord is:

"Come closer in this season and see MY hand in your life like never before. I have new secrets to share with you that will bring you joy."

Have Faith

The word of the Lord is:

"Where is your faith? I have not left you but I am with you at all times. Have faith in ME and know I shall do what I say."

Turn To ME

The word of the Lord is:

"Truth comes by seeking ME and MY word. Turn to ME and learn to hear MY voice. I will give you your options and breakthrough. Seek ME first."

Love Is Your Portion

The word of the Lord is:

"Love is your portion. I increase the love surrounding you. I envelop you in MY love and you shall give love again."

Listen and Be Rewarded

The word of the Lord is:

"The reward is in knowing ME and MY voice. You will find your choices are vast in this season. I will show you the right decisions if you listen."

Fruitful Household

The word of the Lord is:

"Fruitful shall be your household. Open the door and let MY spirit fill your home. Increase is all around you."

Touch MY Spirit

The word of the Lord is:

"Touch MY spirit and agree and you will see miracles set before thee in a greater way. You and I become one today."

Season for Happiness

The word of the Lord is:

"Recognize that I am bringing you strength and wisdom. This is your season for happiness."

Hear ME

The word of the Lord is:

"Pure gold could never be as precious to ME as you. I speak but you don't hear yet I continue to talk to you to get through. Hear ME now victory is yours."

Write It Down, Make It Plain

The word of the Lord is:

"Write it down and make it plain. You are taming your fears in this season. No one can stop you for I have surrounded you in truth and favor."

Plan Ahead

The word of the Lord is:

"Plan ahead for your blessing will come swiftly and your joy will be quick. New beginnings. "

No Looking Back

The word of the Lord is:

"No looking back, this is your time to move forward new laughter is warming a path for new strength and decisions."

Grace and Mercy in Joy

The word of the Lord is:

"Rejoice for I have called you by name to be prosperous. In MY grace and mercy you will find joy and laughter. Glory in MY presence."

Hold Up Your Head

The word of the Lord is:

"You shall witness a breakthrough like never before. Walk with your head up, you have done well and this is your season of reward."

Flow in the Spirit

The word of the Lord is:

"Flow in the spirit and make wise moves in this season. Right connections for new ventures are your portion. Get ready for money making deals."

Perfecting You

The word of the Lord is:

"I am perfecting a thing in you in this season. Trust the process and be patience it will all be worth it."

New Lifestyle

The word of the Lord is:

"Transformation in lifestyle shall be your portion. Get ready for a new release and financial income."

All Things New

The word of the Lord is:

"This is a time for a new approach. You are walking into a new beginning. Rejoice, this is a time of new ideas, new money, and new possibilities."

Fresh Prospective

The word of the Lord is:

"Be mindful of who you share your ideas with. This is your season to do things with a fresh prospective."

Financial Breakthrough

The word of the Lord is:

"Financial breakthrough is banging on your door. Get ready you are going to a new level in life and favor."

Closure to a Difficult Season

The word of the Lord is:

"I bring closure to a difficult season and allow you rest. Test your favor and know I am with you."

Walk It Out

The word of the Lord is:

"New transportation will bring new opportunities. Walk it out. Keep an open mind as this shift happens."

Time of Birthing

The word of the Lord is:

"This is a time of birthing. Silence is holy in MY presence. Cherish the silence that brings you closer to ME."

Be Open to Change

The word of the Lord is:

"New places and new faces will grace your life with increase. Be open to change and be willing to grow. Change is good in this time."

Victory at Your Fingertips

The word of the Lord is:

"Victory is in the palms of your hands. Open them up and receive. MY spirit lives within you."

Don't Limit Yourself

The word of the Lord is:

"Growth is all around you. Don't limit yourself or your options. This is your time to shine in new ways."

ACKNOWLEDGMENTS

To my Lord and savior, my source and my creator, you have breathed life into me in so many ways. I can do no less than demonstrate who you are. Thank you father God it is because of you and through that I can do what I do.

To my loving husband who is always there for me and watching out for my best interest. You are a true covering and I thank God he chose you for me. We are a team and it will always be so, know this.

To my readers, supporters, friends, and family if I can't share the word with you I would have to minister to myself, which I do anyway but it is a blessing to serve God and minister to you. May your prayers and wisdom grow stronger as God make your days longer. God bless you and your loved ones.

Special thanks to my mom for teaching me to share my talents and run after my dreams. Thanks for teaching me to be a finisher. I have been lucky to have had you in my life and I hope someday I can be even half the mommy you were to me. I thank the angels that take care of you for me now. Love you always. I plan to keep my promise.

ABOUT THE AUTHOR

Minister Verleiz Lattimore is not your everyday Minister or everyday Prophetess. God has placed a unique calling on her life that is just as unique as the woman and her name. Verleiz is a lover of God, education and the gift of blessing others with the word of the Lord. It is for God's glory and the shear blessing of seeing the word manifest that moves her in the prophetic, to bring change and growth to God's people.

Verleiz is a loving wife and has written many books in different genres. She is a believer in using the gifts that God has given you. "Find what you love and do it until your heart is content. God will do the rest," Minister Verleiz says.

Other books by Verleiz Lattimore

Let Us Bring Order

Continue to read this book for a sample of Let Us Bring Order

Let Us Bring Order Workbook

Coming Soon

Shattered Pieces of Me: Thoughts from a Healing Heart

Prophetic Silence

Don't Forget the Source

For more about Minister Verleiz Lattimore go to

www.MVProphetess.com

Join me out on Facebook

www.facebook.com/mvprophetess

Let Us Bring Order

Verleiz Lattimore, MBA, MED

Dedicated To Alvin Lattimore

Only You!

Table Of Contents

Introduction

Whose Life is This?   1

See Yourself Whole, See Yourself Rich   13

Delete the Negatives   23

Handling and Circulating Your Money   31

Your Own Boss   47

Why Four Streams   55

Money Matters   63

Taste the Success   69

Mediation – Relaxation   75

Mentors and Mentorship   83

Becoming A Mentor   91

New Beginnings   97

ACKNOWLEDGMENTS

Thanks to my mom who is still leading and guiding, you will always be my number one hero.

To my husband, my Alvin, thanks for the support and help, love you to life.

To Bishop E Bernard Jordan, Pastor Debra Jordan, and family, for getting me to the finish line and filling in the gaps.

To my Morgan, Tee- Tee does it all to see you do better.

Also my big brother, thanks for believing in me even when you didn't see the plan.

~*Introduction*~

What goes up has once been down; we should never fear failure because it is only feedback. It is not who you are when you arrive it is what you do when you are on the journey. Success is in the process of creating the success and being willing to take the risks.

Many people never get passed the idea because they never make the first step. Fear of the first step paralyzes individuals into failure. How can you know what you are capable of if you don't try? You have thankfully made a first step by purchasing this book. Congratulations! You get in life what you invest in and you are a great investment. All you need is to invest your thoughts into your true potential and success.

I believe I can help you met your goals because I have come to understand the model of success. I have come to a place in life where success is magnetized to me the same way I know I can show you to magnetize success to you. I believe in your ability to change your life into the one you have imagined therefore I want to give you the keys I know will insure you the success you desire. I know that reading this book will be an eye opener for you and after you do so you will begin to feel the world open up to you. In addition, by going to www.LetUsBringOrder.com you will gain access to more tools, resources and the complete Let Us Bring Order system that will invoke your success.

If I can share but one secret to success with you while we take this journey together I can offer you the keys to freeing your mind to accomplish anything your heart desires. I can assure you this book will renew your mind as I offer you these tested truths, so that I can do as life does and give to the giver.

I want to take this journey with you because I believe in sharing what I have learned. At the age of thirty-one I find that just the right information and the right amount of risk can help you to move forward. I took a risk when I went to college for Fashion Design and acquired an Associate's Degree. I took another risk when I went on to get my Bachelor's in Education and Psychology. I turned around and took yet three more risks when I went from my MBA in Marketing and Project Management, to my MED in Curriculum Design and Instructional Technology and then another Bachelor's in Metaphysics. All of these risks paid off in the end because they gave me specialized knowledge that has help to build my businesses and ideas. It may not make sense to some but all my risks make sense to my plans and goals, which help to create www.RennyConsulting.com.

I found what I loved in life and pursued a means to make it all work together for my success. You too can find what it is you want from life the most and make great things happen for you. It is not about what the world labels you as; it is what you will label yourself as. You have the God given right to create a great life for you and your family.

In these pages you will find your road map to success on your own terms. You will make the links with what will catapult you into your greatest potential. Life is like clay you have to mold the experience you desire. You want change you have to create it, and you are more than able to do so.

This book will help you to once again find your voice, as you begin to feel alive and in control again. You will see yourself for the great, successful person you are. Let begin this journey to the new you together. I want you to decide now whether you are truly ready for change. Do you know you want better? Are you ready to find out how to get better?

Are you ready to be set free? If you have said yes to all of these questions I want you to begin to make a promise to yourself. Write in the space below, **YES I CAN!!!!!** And sign your name.

_____

(Signed here for your success)
You have just promised yourself success. We shall find the hidden treasure within you. Let Us Bring Order!

So The Journey Begins

~Whose Life is This?~

Chapter One

One of the first steps to moving forward in your life is to ask yourself, *who's life is this?* Are you living the life you want or a life planned by someone else? When you look in the mirror of your life are you seeing something or someone you like? Many of us wander the earth for years following the blueprint that someone else has drawn, never fulfilling the actions that are in the blueprints that are given to us for our own dreams. Hearing the voice of another and not listening to the voice of our own experience.

So once again I ask, *who's life is this?* Are you living the life you want or living the life that someone has planned for you? If you are seeking this book you are probably living someone else's plan however you have realized you are ready to live the life planned by you. So first, it is time for you to sit down and find out what is in this plan of yours. Who do you want to be in life, what do you want to see manifest? What is it you feel you want to accomplish? What is your inner voice saying to you?

The reason planning is so important is that it literally directs your path, without a vision the people parish. If you feel like you are vanishing, then you have failed to focus in on the vision for your life. Goals are the key. I always advise my clients to start by listing ten goals. These are the goals that line up your plan; they are the foundation of your blueprint. You need to make these goals solid and treat them as anchors for your life. You should also be mindful of the goals you are setting because these are truly those things that will carry you to the next level. So list things that hold meaning and truly hold your hearts desires.

Most clients want the new home, the husband or wife, or the successful financial life. These are goals that will motive positive outcomes. Change comes through and from motivation. What will motive you? What goals will cause you to get in gear and really work at the increase in your happiness? These are the goals you start with no matter how large they are, the bigger the dream the more motivation. You see greatness is waiting dormant in you, waiting for you to plan for it to come out. It is not waiting for your best friend to say it is there or for your parents to give it direction. ***It is waiting for you!*** You have to live your own life, you have to give yourself permission to move in the things that life has for you.

Why limit yourself? Tap into those goals that take you into your dreams. If you are working in an office right now in your dream occupation and you have two supervisors above you, make it your business to see yourself in the top position. That should be your goal. No matter if you are not educated enough or if you are not outgoing enough. These are things you can change, and these things change by first setting the goals to change them. The larger the goals the more you can change.

Many of us fear change. Let me first state that fear is totally useless. Fear will kill the dream, the vision and the goals. Face your fear first! The best way to face fear is by saying to yourself, "this is my life, and I am not going to take it anymore." Then take the first action that will lead you to the goal you desire. Success takes willingness and the ability to take risks. Taking action puts you in the state of believing you can do. You have now stepped around fear into the position to decide that you are going to hold the vision you have your heart set on.

Change is also challenging to some, but change will create the new you, the new life. Change is necessary; you will not be the same person you are today when you create the life you truly want. If the you, you are today could make this all happen you would not need to read about getting to where you want. Be it a small change or a very big change, you will change. Change is nothing to fear, I look back on the old me and smile today because I love the new me; the growth, the strength, the creation of opportunity. I've taken the idea of a makeover to the next level. I now look, feel and sound like the part I want to play in life.

Having a plan and setting goals will create a happier, healthier you. You will not have time to worry, only time to see your goals through, time to move toward the new improved life you have mapped out. Having a road map also helps when the Naysayers and the protagonist show up. Those who begin to notice the change and decide it is their duty to tell you, you are going to fail. Come to the table with your head held high. "This is my plan and I am sticking to it." So what goals 1 through 5 are a long shot and they can't see you making them happen. Well guess what, I may not know you half as well as they do but I think you can make every single last one of your goals happen and I think you should try thinking just a bit bigger. Texas is definitely on to something with "bigger is better."

You have to learn to live life for you. It is your world, now you create it. If you have always wanted to open a coffee shop and you make a mean cup of Joe, **HELLO**! Start the goals you need to set to live the life of a coffee shop owner. You have to find the life within your mind that creates the most joy. Little do you know the universe is waiting for you to find this harmony. Your health, wealth and happiness are tied to one thing, your true desire to live your dreams. Successful men and women love what they do and guess what they made plans to get there and are making plans in order to stay there. You can go to www.letusbringorder.com where I have provided tools and resources I want to share with you to help you make these plans and accomplish your dreams!

Here is something else to think on. If you won't help plan your life someone else will. Think about it. All you husbands that did not want to plan the wedding, your mother, mother-in-law and wife were more than happy to plan the whole thing. Some of you may have gotten lucky and had food you enjoyed that day and a tux that you really liked or did not mind, but some unlucky gentlemen ended up with a menu he was sure was not from this world and he was forced to wear a pink bow tie that to this day makes him look at his wife funny each time he remembers or catches a glimpse of the wedding pictures. We can joke about this but it is true. The choice not to plan leaves decisions made that are not in favor of the true vision. You want to know why because someone had a vision and someone else did not, when you have no vision you are volunteering to play a role in someone else's plan. I don't know about you but I like to be a part of the decision making not a part of the after affect.

We have choices; we can choose to feel successful and become successful or feel like losers and become losers. Yes, it is that simple. In every business or business plan the company has goals and a mission. That is every successful business or business plan. What makes you think that your life or your business is any different? Think about the last vacation you went on. Did you plan it? How did it go? It probably sucked big time if you did not plan it or let someone else plan the whole thing. Make the choice to plan your life, to organize what it is you want and desire.

So now some of you are excited. Okay that is great, but you just deflated yourself because you started to think about the money. **STOP**! Do you even know how many people have made plans first and find the money later. You cannot let something so small stop your elevation. Yes, I said something so small. Money is the least of your worries at this point. Okay some of you are ready to throw this book at me because you are looking at some serious financial situations, but you can relax. My goal is to get you to see pass the money for a moment. Yes, money is my friend and I treat my friends very, very well, but my friends don't master me I master them.

If you sit and look at the money you don't have, you are also looking at the money you won't have. You are destroying yourself; you are cutting off the future before the vision has even hit the page. Trust me the plan will bring the money. The plan makes the dream real, and then the dream begins to become alive. You have got to plan in order to put things in order, in order to gain a prospective. You know it is the prospective that awards you the goal. Once you understand your vision and expand it on paper you have expanded and created it in your imagination. This is where it takes shape and form, where it gains life. Now that it has that life in you, you are ready to share it with others. You see these goals for you so clearly and you are able to articulate them so well now people are excited to help you and your vision. They want to give any help they can to move you forward.

For example, let's say you want to go to school to get your marketing degree. You have set the goal; write it down, research the schools both off and online that would be best for you and now you need to fund the dream. You are talking to some friends at a dinner party sharing your passion for your new idea and your dream to make it happen. Jackpot, as you are telling your story someone at the table just came into some extra cash and they are so excited about the plans you have made they want to help. Oh yes, this happens, I have been on both ends of this scenario the help and the helper, and each time the vision was there.

Plan, Plan, Plan! What about the staff? *Plan!* What about the office? *Plan!* What about the funding? *Plan!* What about the car note? *Plan!* My girlfriend/boyfriend thinks this is a stupid idea. *Plan*! They are probably just mad they did not think of it first or they are afraid that you will succeed, and in that case, goal number one should be to replace them in the morning. I was taught not to chase, but replace.

If someone does not fit the vision don't stop dreaming. You find out if they have a real place in the dream and if not guess what replace them. No love lost, you are just working on your happiness, your time to shine. You know half the people in your life right now may not fit into your plan, but again I ask you, *who's life is this?* Are you living for them or for you? Trust me if someone put a million dollars in their hand and said the only condition to keeping the money was walking away from you, they would run. Don't believe me let's start a game show. We can call it love 'em or leave 'em. This is not to say that you are going to be alone at the top, that saying is such a myth. You are never alone at the top the others are just in the background cheering you on. You will meet with your right connections as your goals and plans begin to take shape. Release the dead weight and move forward with the plan.

The key to claiming your life back and creating order and happiness is planning. Then the next step is to place action to that plan. Step out look into what it takes to make each goal move toward success and completion. Then begin to take those steps one by one. Soon you will turn around and need to create all new steps and plans because you will find all the old ones are complete. So as you remember that this is your life, see the vision, write it down, and listen to your heart. It can all be yours, therefore you should be living your dreams, begin to plan begin to hold the vision.

Find out what happens next go to
www.LetUsBringOrder.com

Or Get your copy at Amazon